LOVE IN A
TIME
OF
PESTILENCE

HEATHER GODDIN

LOVE IN A TIME OF TIME OF PESTILENCE

Matador
Unit E2 Airfield Business Park,
Harrison Road, Market Harborough,
Leicestershire. LE16 7UL
Tel: 0116 2792299
Email: books@troubador.co.uk
Web: www.troubador.co.uk/matador
Twitter: @matadorbooks

ISBN 978 1803132 136

British Library Cataloguing in Publication Data.
A catalogue record for this book is available from the British Library.

Printed and bound in Great Britain by 4edge Limited
Typeset in 11pt Minion Pro by Troubador Publishing Ltd, Leicester, UK

Matador is an imprint of Troubador Publishing Ltd

For my beloved Christer,
November 1937 – July 2021

"Love in a time of pestilence."

Poems written or compiled during
lockdowns 2020 / 2021

IN LOCKDOWN

This feels like being in prison,
Solitary confinement at that.
I was never designed for self-isolation
And have no one with whom to share it.

I don't do the evils of technology
But my telephone has now become
My closest friend
And I can keep in touch
With others in like case.

But there is nothing that can help
With the loss of seeing you,
Two thousand miles away and vulnerable
In a place where now I cannot go.
Oh yes, I can still hear your voice,
We can continue to talk
But I cannot kiss your cheek
Or feel your arm in mine
And worst of all
I cannot see your smile.

And always, the ever-present fear
That the longer that this lasts,
The greater the chances are
That I may never see again
That lovely, lovely smile.

March 2020

POPPIES

On the phone, I said,
"My poppies are just coming out."
"Really," you said. "Are they gay?"
"Oh, very bright and gay," said I.
"A brilliant scarlet red."
And then the penny dropped,
My mind's eye saw that wicked grin of yours
That always makes me smile.

"The first bright yellow rose
From the climber on the wall
Has just come out as well," I said.
"Perhaps that's gay as well."

Small crumbs of humour
In this present nightmare world
In which we find ourselves.
Thank God, we can still laugh
At silly things.

May 2020

WILD BIRD IN A CAGE

Long ago in Malta
I had a friend, a formidable lady
Who lived in a pretty cottage
With a glorious garden
Filled with wonderful flowers and trees.
A haven for birds.

Sometimes when she went to England
She would invite me to stay there
To keep an eye on the house,
Let in the gardener in the morning
And feed the feral cats at night.
She gave her maid a holiday
And what little there was to do
I did gladly, for I loved the place.

Once I came home early and found in the garden
The husband of the maid with a robin in a cage,
Set as a lure to catch some other birds.
Furious, I berated him, threatened him with exposure
(My hostess was the Chairman of the Maltese SPB!).
"Your wife could lose her job," I said.
He gave a puzzled smile.
"Oh, but he happy. He sing," he said.
"He doesn't sing for joy," said I.
"He sings because he wants to fly
And warns the others not to come.
He wants to be free."

I left a short time after
And do not know what followed.
When I returned his wife still had her job.
The robin was safer where it was.
Its wings were clipped. It could not fly.
It never would be free.

I, too, am now
A wild bird in a cage
Wings clipped, unable to fly.
I keep on singing in my cage
But not for joy,
Wanting my freedom,
Wanting to fly,
To be with someone that I love.

April 2020

VIRTUAL HUGS

Some days are worse than others
Or better
Depending on how you look at it.

We now depend on virtual hugs
Or socially-distanced smiles.
The kiss of the sun can help
Or the comfort of warm shade
But lowering skies and rain
Depress the spirits further.

I swing between hope and despair
But what I really want
Is to lean my head against your shoulder
And weep.

But I cannot do that either.

May 2020

SMALL PLEASURES

I try to count my blessings.
Lockdown's not all bad.
At least I have a garden
Where I can sit and watch the world go by.
I see people passing on the road.
Real people who can wave and smile.

Halfway down the street on my permitted walk
There is a wooden bench
On which I sit to rest my feet,
On a daisy-splattered green.
Here I can listen to the sighing of the wind
In the tall pines in a wood across the road.
I can hear the birdlife all around.
The rusty screech of pheasant,
Murmuring collar doves,
Chaffinch, blackbird, chiff-chaff, tit,
The songs we take for granted
And often scarcely hear.

Sitting in sunshine in the garden of my home
I study insects passing by my chair,
Living active insects on business of their own.
Black or golden beetles, ladybirds and busy ants
Noisy bumblebees, elegant stripey-sweatered wasps.
Even the nasty blowfly has its charm
In its body-suit of bright metallic blue –
I see them all more clearly than before.

And as for flowers and flowering trees,
How often do we find the time
To watch the seasons come and go?
The deep, dark purple lilacs,
Clematis pink or deeply scented white
Tumbling over garden walls.
Wisteria on a neighbour's porch,
Candles on a chestnut tree
And Judas trees in purple bloom.

Soon, the poppies on the verge
Beyond my garden wall
Will burst into a scarlet cloud.
Midsummer daisies will explode
From the grass beside the gate.
Has there ever been such a lovely blossoming spring?

But one simple pleasure isn't small at all.
It's dialling your number,
Waiting for you to lift your phone,
Waiting for the joy of hearing your voice.
Even the answerphone will do
As often you will ring me back.
What *can* be better than that?
Lockdown's not *all* bad.

May 2020

HUMANIST FUNERAL

I had mixed feelings about this.
All my experience was of funerals within a church.
It was winter and wet. Heavy cloud.
But I knew I must go,
For I had loved her and known her for many years
And I needed to pay my last respects
And be there with others to support
The man she'd left behind.

She had loved flowers, nature and children.
The Church had had no place in her life.
But we had always said,
"She is the nicest woman in the village."

So here I stand with others in a little wooded space,
With lifeless trees and wet dead leaves,
Thick-piled beneath our feet,
The simple coffin and the open grave.
The rain had stopped,
But it was '*dreich*' and cold.

Yet in that simple service
Something happened in that place.
Amidst the words of tribute and the music that she
loved,
Smiling at memories from her loved ones
And the many friends she'd known,
I felt a lightness rising from within
Banishing for a while
That sense of grief and loss,
A kind of joy in a life well spent
And Christian or not
God was there.

December 2019

HAIRY HORRORS

When they closed the shops,
The libraries, the schools, the pubs,
The cafés and the restaurants,
The piteous cry rang out:
"Oh, what about my roots?"
Hairdressers and the barber shops
Had had to close as well.

The summer promises to show
Some interesting sights
And when we take permitted walks
This village will soon get to know
Who's not a natural blonde.
Our home-made skills will soon emerge
From trigger-happy scissors.
Men wearing hats to hide
Eccentric cuts and shapes
That sadly lie beneath.
Biblical beards will start to grow.
Moses and Methuselah.
Unless they shave them off, of course,
To show the unfamiliar face below.
And for the rest,
Long, flowing tresses, grey or white,
Blowing in the breeze.

My own hair grows like weed
I'll soon be white not blonde.
I'll kid myself that no one else
Will ever spot the difference.
I'll soon become a cross between
A scarecrow and a hairy dog
(Old English Sheepdog breed).
But, thankfully, my fringe will grow
To hide the wrinkles on my brow.

In six months' time,
What then?
Exciting days still lie ahead.

March 2020

OASIS

Sometimes I look at the distance between us
Not as fields and woods and northern seas,
A place of temperate heat and cooling rains,
But as a desert of unending, shifting sands.
Whilst on the horizon I can see
The shimmering image of a green oasis.

A place of calm and healing hands,
Of water and of sustenance,
Where I may lie down to rest and sleep,
To dream of friendship and of love.

You are my green oasis,
Just out of sight beyond the drifting sands.
Putting all doubts aside,
I shall walk on with resolution
Towards the reality of where you are.

March 2010 / Revised May 2020

CAPTIVE HEART

You have stolen away my heart
What will you do with it?

Will you keep it safe in a box?
Take it out from time to time
To look at it?
Will you set it on a plinth, on show,
And treasure it?
Will you place it, like a tame dove,
In a gold cage, to feed from your hand?
Never in a thousand years.
That's not your style.

Maybe you'll despise and reject it.
Use it as a punchbag, perhaps,
Or bounce it like a tennis ball
Along the ground?
Would you use it for target practice?
Or, even more bizarrely,
Stuff it, cook it, eat it?
(You might not like the taste. It's very old and tough.)
More likely you will add it to the pile
Of all the other hearts you've stolen,
Piled in a heap in some dusty corner.
But would you really do these things?
Not even you, I think.

Even if you break it
(By accident or design),
Roughly mended with sticky tape
Or held together with string,
It will survive
And go on loving you.

May 2020

BOUQUET OF PHEASANTS

Lockdown means less traffic on the road,
So local pheasants have all thrived this spring.
From early March, competing males
Have screeched their songs from dawn to dusk,
Awakened me at early light and stopped me
Dozing off at night.
Like headless chickens, flocks run around the roads
When I take my early morning walk.
Accompanied me with raucous cries and whirring
wings.
The alpha male, resplendent in his mating robes,
Is followed round by concubines in droves.
Rejected suitors hang around
Waiting for their chance.

By now there must be many nests
In fields and gardens everywhere.
Next year could see
An even bigger bouquet in the street.

But once the lockdown ends…
What then?

May 2020

MARKING TIME

I sit in the sun, outside the house,
Watching the roses blowing in the wind
And I think that here I am again
Wishing my life away. Just marking time.

All the time I grow older and less able.
How many years do I have left to live?
How many seasons more are there for me?
How long before I see your face again
Other than in dreams and photographs?

The roses will fade and the autumn leaves will fall.
Stepping stones across a river
That I cannot yet cross
And all the while I wait.
Just marking time. Wishing my life away.

June 2020

ANCIENT RITUALS

There are so many ancient customs
But the Swedish ones are different.
Sometimes a trifle bizarre.
Decidedly odd to British eyes.
One shouldn't be surprised,
They're Vikings after all!

I remember a Crayfish Party
To celebrate the summer's end,
Which once you made for me.
Patterned paper hats and aprons.
A tablecloth to match with pictures of the fish.
It can become quite messy,
Tearing off shells to get to the flesh,
Sucking the juices out of the heads,
Washing all down with glasses of beer
And plenty of schnapps.
The merrier it gets the more they sing songs,
The words of which I don't understand
But they sound to me like rugby songs.

Next it's time for Glögg,
A Yuletide treat
Which makes mulled wine
Resemble warmed-up apple juice.
I know because I've watched it made.
Half bottles of wine. A lot of brandy.
All kinds of spices. A sugar cone.
And a *bottle* of vodka.

And then the show begins.
Pure theatre. A spectacle.
Mixture is heated, poured over the cone
Precisely and slowly
And then set on fire.
A firework show of great intensity.
We watch entranced until the fire goes out
To rounds of applause.
It's poured into tiny glass cups.
Teaspoons of nuts and dried fruit
Go into the mix.
It's rather sweet and seems quite innocuous
Until you have drunk quite a lot.
When life becomes different and everyone's happy.

Dear Master of the Home-Made Schnapps.
Oh Wonderful Wizard of Glögg
What's next?
I'm on a learning curve.

January 2020

FUTILE DREAMS

I often wish that I was rich.
So rich, in fact, that I could grant
The wishes of some people most in need.
To be an unknown friend who works a miracle.

Paying off a mortgage, cancelling a debt.
Helping with an illness or a holiday.
Uniting friends and families
In some far, distant land.
To leave to someone that I love
Something worthwhile.

But I am poor
And I cannot play God.
I cannot even realise
My own quite hopeless dreams.

But dreams,
Where would we be without them?
We need them to stay alive.

June 2020

WISHES

I want to be your umbrella,
To shield you from rain and from harm.
I want to bring you some laughter
And never cause you pain.

I want to peel your potatoes,
Wash up the pans in your sink.
Sweep up the dust from all of your corners.
Be the carpet under your feet.

I want to be the light
At the end of your tunnel,
Share all your burdens and fears,
Build you a shelter from wind and from snow
And catch you if ever you fall.

If you reach out to me
I want to be there.

May 2020

PROMISES

The more I come to know you
The more I see your layers of complexity.
Your proud and independent spirit.
You never let anyone get too close,
You need your space far more than most.
That I respect and understand
For I, too, need my space.

I promise,
I will try to never crowd you.
I will never make demands
And ask no more of you
Than you can freely give.

But if ever you need me
I will be there.

June 2020

NIGHTINGALES

I do not have much choice
For a "healthy walk" in lockdown
Within the confines of the village.
Up to the pub, which now is closed.
Down to the church, which now is locked.
Some variations now devised.
A circular tour around the new estates
Or downhill to the nursing home.

Today I've walked further than before,
I took another road I hadn't walked
For fifteen years or more.
And as I went, a memory wakened from the past
That this was a place where nightingales had sung,
All day long and through the night.
And as I reached those long-remembered trees
A nightingale began to sing
In full and glorious song.

So beautiful that sound becomes
When it offers love songs to the moon and stars.
No competition from the nightjars and the owls.
But when it sings all through the day
It seeks to put all other birds to shame.
Doubles its efforts to eclipse them all.
Chaffinch, blackbird, thrush and wren
And a mighty chorus of the other birds as well.
It has to work for it and wins top prize.

When I returned the song had ceased
But I had had my moment of delight.
Some things are still the way they were.

In this place, at this time,
Lockdown isn't lockdown
Anymore.

June 2020

THE RIVER

The journey has been long and hard,
So many almost unsurmountable hills
And deep, dark, sunless valleys.
I've known moments of terror
On rough and treacherous ground
But I have strived and prevailed.
And on smooth roads I have dared to hope.
I have never lost faith.

But now, when I have almost reached my goal,
I am confronted by a river
Too deep and wide to swim across.
Had I wings I would fly,
If I had time I would find a boat
Or build a bridge.
But time is short
And I am powerless in the face of things.

On the distant shore I can see people
Gathering to meet me,
You, amongst them, waving me on.
Can no one help me cross?

I pace the shore,
Praying for a miracle.
I say, again and again,
"Can no one help me cross?"

June 2020

IMPLANTS

When he rang today, he said,
"I've had six teeth extracted
And now I've shocked my dentist."

"What *did* you say?" I asked.
And he replied, "I told him that I hoped
He'd keep the implant costs in check,
As in a year or two
I'll be going to the furnace
And it all seems such a waste."

"I hope he laughed," said I.
"Yes, in a rather startled way," he said.
"I've sixteen implants now
And all the kronor I have ever saved
Are now inside my mouth.
I should be worth a fortune."

"Then make the most of it," I said.
"Live and enjoy each day.
It isn't everyone who can say
I've put my money where my mouth is."

June 2020

CHRISTMAS AT JUAN DE LA COSA, SANTONA, 2019

Last night on Christmas Eve
They shut the bar at half-past nine
To let the staff go early to their homes
To celebrate with families and friends.
Before he left, the barman brought free drinks,
Bottles of some local wines,
Some quite unknown and others that we knew
And Spanish brandy with its pinkish glow.

After a time and one by one
We all drew nigh to test our legacy
And tried a glass or two
(Or three or four), for some drank more than others.
Some potions were innocuous. Others quite disgusting.
Some I might even try again.
The evening was convivial.
Friendships were formed.
And we were filled with Christmas cheer.

Some went early to their beds,
Others lingered on.
By the time I left
We were down to four or five,
The hardened core.

But as far as I know
No one "wrecked the joint"
Or drank the bottles dry.
I slept soundly through the night,
Came early to my breakfast.
The trolley and the glasses
Had all been cleared away.
The room was clear
And no one was left snoring
In a comfortable chair.

Christmas Day 2019

LANDFALLS AND FAREWELLS

I stand in the gardens high above the harbour
In the clear, bright air of spring,
Watching for the plane
That will take you far away.

So many landfalls and farewells in my life.
All those I've loved the most
Distanced from me in so many ways,
Away at sea, travelling afar
Or dwellers in another place.

And now I know
That these were just a preparation.
In loving you, my friend,
I have made another landfall
And yet one more farewell
Far greater than the rest.

Malta, April 2009 / Revised 2020

A GATHERING OF LADYBIRDS

There has been an explosion of hoverflies
And now it's the turn of the ladybirds
Emerging from the grass.
Seated on my garden chair
I watch them gathering all around.
I have to be careful where I put my feet.

And then I see a curious thing.
Some kind of deformation on a creature's back.
Curiosity knows no bounds.
I went to fetch a magnifying glass.

What's now revealed is very strange.
A small one sitting on another's back.
I know nothing of the habits of a ladybird.
What *is* this all about?
Mating, attacking or devouring?
Or just a helpful "piggy-back"?
And then they shuffled off,
Back to the grass and out of sight.

Intrigued, I went to fetch a book
With secrets of the insect world.
I know much more about the habits
Of the seven-spot ladybird.
But nothing relevant at all.
What *did* I see?
I still am none the wiser.

May 2020

SUMI JO WITH BLACKBIRD OBLIGATO

On fine, warm days I like to sit
In the shadow of my garage door
With a view of the road and people passing by.

I have come to know the birds
Who nest in the ivy on the wall.
The robin who I'm trying to tame
And the family of fieldmice near the gate
Who skim across the path so fast
They're gone before I've blinked an eye.

Sometimes I play CDs on my player,
Transported to my kitchen.
Not loud enough to be a nuisance
To my neighbours
Or startle rare walkers on the road.

Today I played the voice of Sumi Jo,
Arias and songs from eighteenth-century Italy,
Giordano, Gluck, Caldara.
A blackbird nervously approached
And peered inside my open kitchen door,
Cocked his head and listened, that I swear,
To that exquisite voice
Until he flew to the ivy-covered wall
And sat close by for quite a while.
And then he flew to the topmost branches
Of a nearby tree.
Began to sing, strong and clear,
The melody embellished with runs and little trills,
Competing, I am sure, with that other glorious voice.
Consummate artists both.

He fell silent when the music ceased
And flew away.
The recital was at an end,
Sumi Jo with blackbird obligato.

June 2020

SUMMER RAIN, 2012

Lord, how it rained!
From the moment I arrived
Until the day I left.
The coldest, wettest June for ninety years.
My sunshine came from being there with you.
It didn't matter that the skies were grey
And cold, hard rain came lashing down.

One day we took a coach to Kapellskär
And caught the ferry to the Åland Isles.
It threaded its way between the wooded isles
And lonely skerries, some no more than rocks,
Looming ghostlike through the mist
On leaden, white-capped seas.

I had been to Mariehamn before
And seen the beauty of the islands.
This Swedish-speaking Finnish place.
It didn't seem the right day to return.
So we never went ashore,
Just waited on the ship
And came straight back.

But sitting in the restaurant,
With glasses of good wine
And brightly coloured food on pure white plates,
It felt as though the rain had ceased.

I sat beside you on the coach on our return.
The rain flowed like a river on the road ahead,
I watched you sleep, said to you silently,
The words I could not say aloud.
Then you opened your eyes and smiled
And I felt once more
The absent warmth of the sun.

The day I left the sun came out again
But in my heart the rain began once more.

June 2012 / Revised July 2020

CLEANING OUT CUPBOARDS
AND DRAWERS

At the start of the lockdown I made a resolution
To clear out my cupboards and drawers
And go through the CDs I'd hoarded for years.

The CDs came first,
A daunting experience.
Things I'd forgotten,
A voyage of discovery.

What made me buy *that*?
Or was it a gift?
The ones I'd forgotten
And those that I loved
But mostly unplayed
In the passage of years.

Beethoven, Brahms and Phillip Glass,
Schumann, Vaughan Williams,
Elgar and Bach.

I resurrected from the pile
The singers of my youth.
Jessye Norman, Jussi Björling, Pavarotti.
The living singers, too
Renée Fleming, Joe Calleja, Jonas Kaufmann,
Bringing back memories of arias and songs
That once I sang myself.
A host of folk songs, Scots and Irish.

Two copies of Beethoven's Triple Concerto?
And *two* of Korngold's Violin Concerto?
How can I choose between them?
I'll have to keep them both.

All summer long they've given me
Memories and moments of delight.
I've played them all
And will play them all again.
With the exception of only one or two.

As for the cupboards and drawers,
They can wait.

July 2020

GHARB (APRIL 2016)

Do you remember the last time
That we went to Gharb?
When we took the road uphill
From our favourite church at Ta Pinu,
Crossing the stone-walled valley
With its fertile fields stretching to the sea,
The great shrine of the church on our left
And the Pharos perching on the cliffs to our right.
We climbed the hill to Gharb.
No way as easy as the last time that we came
But we *did* it with a small degree of pride.

We lunched at our favourite restaurant,
Where the owner still remembered us.
A bottle of local wine and lovely food
(Snails and fish, as I remember)
Alone in an old walled courtyard
With climbing vines and welcome shade.

Before we caught our bus
We visited the small, round church
In the middle of the square.
A small bright gem of Baroque art
And as we came inside
A choir began to sing.
Choir practice had begun.

Your arm around my shoulders,
We sat and listened to them sing.
Beautiful music, beautifully sung.
We clapped them when we left.
A sea of smiling faces.
Hands waving us goodbye.

Will we ever climb that hill again?
I doubt it very much.
We could board a bus to Ta Pinu
And on another day a bus to Gharb.
The shrine of Ta Pinu will still be there
But not, perhaps, our restaurant at Gharb
And we'd be very lucky
To stumble on choir practice once again.

But in my heart I know
That we will never go again,
But the memory of that lovely day shines on
Like the Pharos in the dark.

July 2020

ROOM WITH A VIEW

The room was small
And hardly worth the supplement
But the view from the window
Was one for which to die.

A view of bridges, towers and spires,
Of water sparkling in the morning light.
The small, white ships and tourist boats.
A flight of swans across the sun.
The fire of autumn leaves.
Cascades of seagulls tumbled from the roof
In a dazzling, noisy cloud of white
To meet the sea below
And in my heart this bubbling joy
At the thought of seeing you.

But now that I am waiting to depart
The scene is one of monochrome
The colour faded from the view.
Black and white.
Shades of grey.
An autumn sun behind the clouds.
The seagulls seem quite different now,
Tumbling in showers from the roof,
Like grey rocks from a precipice.
Mind and heart fall seaward with them,
At the thought of leaving you.

October 2011

NEOWISE

July was nearly gone
Before I saw the planet,
Time and again the skies were far too cloudy
Or I'd slept through its presence
In the skies.

But the night before last
I tried and failed to get to sleep
And went to make myself a cup of tea.
The sky was clear and spattered lavishly
With a multitude of stars,
And there before my eyes was Neowise.

I made my tea and fetched a chair,
Turned out the light and from my kitchen door
I watched its progress through the skies.
A perfect viewing space.
A lamp bulb lighting up the sky.
Its streaming tail quite clearly seen.
(Millions of years in length, or so I'm told.)
But to the naked eye, just threads of gold.
For several hours I sat quite still,
Striving to watch it move,
Almost imperceptibly, it seemed,
Though when I went away and then returned
I saw quite clearly that it had.

No competition from the firmament.
The planets paled but held their ground.
They put up no resistance.
The stars put up a decent fight,
Sparking a bit from time to time.
And one star paid the ultimate price,
Exploded, died and fell into space.
(That is a bonus for someone like me.
I love to watch a shooting star.)

The comet grew smaller
As it travelled further from the earth,
A mere pinprick of light.
A Will of the Wisp.
("Now you see me. Now you don't.")
Then it disappeared from sight.

I went back to bed and slept.
Before I did I thought in wonder and in awe
Of the wonders of the cosmos,
The mysteries of time and space,
My one and only comet.
It will not be forgotten.

July 2020

SNOW IN STUREGATAN

The night before I left
The snow came down again,
Carpeting the streets in virgin white.
The traffic on the road outside was hushed,
Muffled and strangely sparse.
We ventured out to eat,
My "thank you" for a lovely time.
We had a favourite place close by.
It had to be a special meal,
Good food and wine with silver service.
But there was some kind of Sunday holiday
In the wake of the New Year.
We had forgotten that almost everywhere
Was closed.

We trawled the streets in search of food,
Propping each other up on frozen ground,
Knowing full well that if *one* slipped and fell
The other would fall down as well
And heaven knows how we'd get up
Without a hoist or human aid
And no one was about.
But, happily, we both survived.

One restaurant was open but the place was full
Of Stockholm youth in thrall to TV football games.
(Not our scene at all!)
We tried the hotel round the corner
But all they offered was the usual Sunday fare,
Meatballs, burgers, Skagen toast.
Not good enough, we both agreed.

And then you had a brainwave.
"Do you like Indian?" you said.
"I do, quite well," said I.
So we tottered up the street
And found the place was open.
(When are Indian restaurants *not*?)
The food was quite good,
Enhanced by the best wine that they had.
We dined in a solitary state.

Then back to the street. So beautiful the snow
Sparkling on pavements in the lamplight's glow.
An almost silent world,
Quite alien to the usual busy road.
When we reached our base
I said, "That wasn't too bad, I think."
And we laughed and kissed,
Joyous, light, spontaneous.
The way that happy children do.
The children that inside, we both still are.

You saw me to my door and to the lift
And moments on
We waved to each other
From across the courtyard space.
You from your kitchen, I from my room.
I went to bed happy.
Forgot in sleep about the morrow.

Next day the snow was gone again.
(They don't make winters here the way they used to
do.)
And when I left I took away a little joy,
Remembering the snow in Sturegatan.

January 2019 / Revised January 2020

UNTITLED

When you came you brought back meaning to my life.
Made me aware of things outside myself.
Gave me, in old age, the youth I'd never had.

You have given me laughter, joy and hope
And (dare I say it?)
Sometimes grief.

You have painted pictures in bright colours
Onto the drab canvas of my life.
You have carved images into the stonework of my
memory.
You have swept my empty midnight skies with dancing
light.
You have filled my dreams with stars.

The road that lies behind us isn't long,
The road ahead is shorter still
And it isn't long enough.
I am only too aware that all too soon
You may be gone.
And I shall lose what gives a meaning to my life.

But you will not go lonely to your grave,
For the part of me that is *me*
Will go with you.

September 2019

SAXMUNDHAM DOGS

I think that now I know them all,
The vast community of dogs
Who live around my local market town.

Thoroughbreds, mongrels, rescue dogs.
All shapes and sizes, beautiful or cute
And sometimes neither.
Big dogs, long legs, thick curly coats, expressive eyes.
The tiny ones. Short legs and fringes to the nose and
cuddly sweet.
Smooth-coated ones. Vociferous.
Old dogs with stiff, arthritic joints
And puppies, loving everyone, frolicking around.
All share the same sharp-focused quest,
The jar of biscuits just inside the door.

We sit outside The Gallery,
Socially distanced with our coffee cups
In the tiny space beside the road,
Inhaling petrol fumes, in sun and shade,
And here they come, the local dogs
(Mitzi, Buster, Dylan, Luna, Dreyfer,
Naming just a few).

And visitors from other towns (word gets around)
Come trotting up, all straining at the leash.
They don't forget. Won't pass the door
Without they seek dear Michael with his magic jar
Of tempting canine treats.
He never lets them down.
I always say to new folk on the scene,
"You'll never get your dog to pass this door again
Without they get their treat."

When Gary brings their spaniel, George
(The master of this place),
He nearly knocks me off my chair
With wriggling rump and truncheon-tail
And paws that do not know their strength.
But when he's quietened down again
He sits upon my feet and keeps them warm.
He gets his share of biscuits, too.
Who can resist those pleading eyes?

I can't think of a nicer place to be
In Covid semi-isolation
Than on the high street in Saxmundham
With coffee and with friends,
Making the acquaintance of local, friendly dogs.

September 2020.

FRUIT FLY

After a day of ferocious heat
I sat in the garden with a glass of wine.
A tiny fruit fly came and dived into my drink,
Lured by the scent of wine.

Three choices were now given to me.
Fish him out and stamp on him?
Try to save him? Drink him down?
I wasn't prepared to throw the wine away
And sacrifice my ration for the day.

I fished him out and set him on a fingertip,
Prostrate in a pool of alcohol.
I thought at first that he was dead.
But when I saw him twitch a leg
I sat with finger in the air
Until the wine had dried
And then he moved his legs and flexed his wings.

I took a blade of grass to help him with his take-off,
But not quite ready for the task ahead,
He fell into my lap instead.
Totally pissed, he ran around in circles for a bit
Then spread his wings and flew away.
He flew a zig-zag course, no doubt,
But, against all odds, he had survived
And lived to drink another day.

I finished up my glass of wine.

August 2020

CHRISTMAS LUNCH 2020

The time approached I dread the most
The loneliness of Christmas
Without a family
Or the friends I love the most.
In lockdown, far, far worse.
No wonder that in normal times
I go away to spend the days
With others in like case.

But in these dark and troubled times
I made a vow to make good use
Of ways to celebrate alone.
Good food, good wine
And ways to keep a smile upon my face.

I laid four places on a pure white cloth,
My favourite mats and coasters,
Best china and most precious glass,
Linen napkins edged with Maltese lace,
A centrepiece of candles and some Christmas flowers.

My toys drew lots amongst themselves
For who would share my feast.
(They may have cheated, I suspect,
For those who won were favourites.
A reindeer and two polar bears.)

Roger the Reindeer sat upon my left
I worried that I didn't have the lichen that he eats
But he seemed quite happy with green vegetables instead.
The polar bears sat on my right and shared a chair,
Not because they're joined together at the hip
But just because they're brothers
And Per, the elder, likes to keep an eye
On little Christer, making sure that he behaves.
I had no qualms about their meal,
Turkey or smoked fish are all the same
To carnivores like polar bears.

The meal went well,
Their table manners were impeccable.
They never said a word.
Switched off their mobile phones.
Listened politely to the CDs that I played,
Svenson, Grieg and Alfvén from their northern lands.

They left clean plates and never touched the wine.
I didn't have much washing-up to do.

The chair across from me was empty
But I placed your photo facing me
On the snowy tablecloth.
Your smile shone out at me
From its shiny, silver frame
And I raised my glass to you from time to time,
Pretended you were there.

I actually enjoyed myself,
For I had company of sorts.
The food was good.
The wine was even better.
I may be mad
But the whole thing kept me sane.

January 2021

THE MOUSE THAT ROARS

I am the mouse that roars in the face of Covid-19.
I stand strong. Face up to it.
Refuse to be reduced to a paranoid neurotic
Like others I see around me.
We have to live with this for who knows how long.

Yes, I obey the rules.
I take no risks. Nor risk others.
I wear my mask. I distance.
Wash my hands and sanitise
Dozens of times a day.
But I fight back in the presence of a monster.

I put my faith in God.
I am not afraid.
For others, yes, but not for myself.

I accept my vaccination
With grateful thanks.
A step in the right direction
Onto a path that leads us out of a nightmare.
The path that will take me
Towards the place where I'll see you again.

January 2021

FAMILY

They said (I hope not out of spite
But thoughtlessly),
"I suppose you don't fear Covid
Because you have no family for whom to care."
Words that stabbed me to the heart
Because that's not my fault.

I have no living soul to call my own.
No children and no siblings.
Parents, cousins, long since gone,
I have no living ties of blood.
My friends are now my family.
Perhaps that is a blessing,
For we choose them
And they choose us.

The friend that I love most
Is father, brother, child to me.
My anchor and my rock,
But he is old and frail and far away,
And yes, I fear for him.
There are so many friends now
That I know
I'll never see again.
My family grows smaller all the time.

So don't think that I don't fear Covid.
I *do* but only for my much-loved friends,
Who're all the family I need.

February 2021

COVID-19

Now I have looked it in the eye,
It has caused me sleepless nights,
Waiting for news of you.
I have looked from a cliff edge
Into the abyss
And I have prayed a lot.

Not knowing is worse than knowing the worst
But against all odds you have survived.
When you rang to tell me you were home
I felt I rose from deep, dark waters
Onto calm seas and brilliant light.
Thanks be to God.

March 2021

SNOW MOON

I tossed and turned. Unable to sleep.
At last I rose and went to the kitchen,
Treading a silver path to my door,
Where the full moon, silver-white, rode a cloudless sky,
Made tea and sat in chilly quiet,
Calming my fears
In what seemed like daylight night.

Then I went back to bed and slept
But still I woke early before the sun came up.
By now the moon had travelled far,
Hung like a giant bauble in the west
Silver gilt, touched by the first rays of the sun,
Rising in the east.
Its lakes and mountains clearly defined.

I wanted to take it down
And place it in your hands.
An elixir for your sickness,
Lowering your fever, soothing away your pain,
Bathing you in its life-giving waters
Lifting your soul in its heavenly light.

They tell me it is called the Snow Moon.
In a nightmare Covid world
I call it Hope.

February 2021

GREEN TOMATO JAM

When you rang I said,
"I have this day
Finished your jar of green tomato jam."
(One of the jars you've given me
Over the past few years
Of your lovely marmalade and jam.)
"I've rationed it," I said,
"Because who knows how long the time
Before we meet again."

"Meanwhile I'll wash the pot and label it.
Your name, the contents and the year,
To join the other rows of empty jars
Stacked at the back of a cupboard
In my kitchen.
I know you think I'm raving mad
But that is how it is," I said.

"Oh yes, I do," you said,
"But I've got used to it."

Somehow I find that comforting.
I don't know why?
But yes, it is.

March 2021

MAGIC CARPETS

All through the lonely days of lockdown
I have thought often about Malta,
Remembering the places that we knew and loved.
A hotel on the bastions like *Fawlty Towers*,
Small, dark rooms and dreadful food.
Reception staff we knew as friends.
The dear, old waiters in the dining room.
"Speedy Gonzalez" the chambermaid,
Who took all day to clean ten rooms.
Where we started each day at breakfast
With that view of Grand Harbour
That never failed to take our breath away.
It was our very special place.
We loved it for itself.

Ancient buses held in place
With super glue and string?
The windows that would never close.
(We needed umbrellas in our seats
When the autumn rains began to fall.)
Drivers unheeding of the Highway Code.
(All picked for charm and courtesy?)
Surly and glum yet volatile,
Throwing tantrums if put out
By passengers or other drivers on the road.

Our favourite restaurants
Beside the sea or on Mdina's silent streets.
The bars and cafés in Valletta's bustling heart,
So many now long gone.

Concerts at the Manoel.
The services within our favourite church.
Walking Valletta's crowded daytime streets,
Yet strangely quiet at night.
Meeting up with well-loved friends
Who are no longer there.

My memories go further back than yours.
An ancient house in a narrow street
With Roman foundations and a well in the dining room.
A spiral staircase to the roof
And several ghosts.
Cold and damp in winter. Buckets placed to catch the leaks
And yet for years it was the centre of my world.

The waggon roads, the footpaths through the fields,
I walked them all,
Through villages where friendly people greeted me
And life was safe and innocent.
One never had to lock a car or door.
Will we ever go again?

I doubt it very much
Unless we take our magic carpets to the place
Transporting us from door to door.
Would we even know it now?
With progress and technology
Has come the loss of innocence.

Big, new hotels. New buses (much improved?).
Congested traffic, petrol fumes,
Paved roads where once the footpaths ran.
Plenty of crime and violence.
Cars and doors now firmly locked.

And where now would we find the space
To park the magic carpets
Safely and unlocked?
For the moment that we turned our backs
Someone would nick them both
To sell upon their market stall.

But still it casts its spell on us
Not yet like everywhere else.
Evil lurks beneath the skin,
It always has and always will.
It's not just there but everywhere.
A warm and friendly people haven't really changed.
The island is still beautiful
And we will love it all our days.

May 2021

SHRINKAGE

There are those who say that flowers scream in silent
pain when picked
And vegetables groan in agony when wrenched from
their bed of earth.
(Not good news for veggies and vegans!)
Now I hear similar things about our clothes.
Post-lockdowns we're finding they're now too small.
We haven't put on weight. In fact, they've *shrunk*.

Tucked away in cupboards or drawers,
Neglected and depressed, they've pined away from lack
of use.
We don't go out the way we used to do.

I can't say that is true for me.
I ring the changes all the time.
(I dress up even if I can't go out.)
I open my cupboards, stir them round
And talk to them.
(There's no one else with whom to talk.)
And all of them still fit.
They haven't shrunk at all.

I cannot say the same for shoes,
For when I tried them in a shop
They fitted well, were comfortable
But when I got them home and wore them in the street
They always gave me hell.
They languish on their shelves.
I ought to throw them out to give them life
But still I don't, because I hope
That next time that I try them out they'll suit me very
well,
Despite dropped arches, swollen feet and twisted toes.
Shoes sometimes fit and sometimes don't.

I have neglected them.
My shoes have shrunk.
A fitting punishment, I think.

May 2021

LOST TREASURES

I woke from a dream in which I found
My missing treasure trove.
But the moment of joy was quickly gone
And left me with that ever-present sense of loss.
A paper package full of memories,
Precious to no one but myself.

A carrier bag of cards and letters
That you sent me long ago.
Concert programmes that I kept.
The sling you gave me when I broke my wrist.
A ticket stub from a steam-train trip from Mariefred.
A letter that is better lost
Although I know it off by heart.
The birthday card you sent
In the days before your illness took away
Your writing skills.
Each year my birthday came around
I took it out to join the others on the shelf
Knowing that you couldn't send another.

Where these treasures went I'll never know.
Swept out with piles of papers to the rubbish bin?
I've searched the house and never found a thing.
I lost them many months ago
And still I grieve for them.

But are they *really* lost?
They will be there inside my head.
Invisible, intangible, they'll still be there
As long as I can keep my wits
And they'll *still* be with me when I die.

June 2021

"GRIEF IS THE PRICE WE PAY FOR LOVE."

There is a moment when I wake from blessed sleep
When everything seems normal.
I think, "I'll ring you later on today,"
And then I remember
You are no longer there.

I think of your empty rooms
(The rooms I'll never see again).
The pictures on the walls, the crystal chandelier.

The old, worn, leather sofa near the window.
White china cups with golden rims from which we
drank our tea.
The little artefacts you loved.
And a silver snuff box that I gave you several years ago.

I'm glad now that I took the narrow corridor
Between two lockdowns in the autumn of last year
When I was happy just to be with you.
I went to church with you.
We went to shop for food to buy to eat
And stayed indoors to cook and eat it, drink good wine.
We listened to music, watched TV.
Sometimes we went to favourite restaurants.
We talked about things we'd do the next time that I came.
Covid seemed lightyears away.
I am richer for that last week that I spent with you.

I think of the plans we had
To travel to the island that we loved,
With a good and trusted friend.
You and I and Mats.
Would it have happened?
Probably not but the dream was there
And it is our dreams that keep us strong.

Your phones ring on in an empty space
And for a while, I can still hear your voice
Until they disconnect them both.
But these are early days. I bleed inside.
He was the other half of me. I am no longer whole.
There is no joy in anything.

Now I must find my way ahead
For Death is part of life. You told me many times.
But nothing can calm the aching grief.
I promised you once that I wouldn't be depressed,
That I would laugh at life the way *you* always did,
But that is hard, for the tears are formed,
Although they'll never fall.
For never again will I feel your arm in mine,
The warmth of your hand,
The soft skin of your cheek beneath my kiss
Or see again your wondrous smile.

I am glad that I am old,
For the years go faster all the time.
Nothing worse can happen to me now.

July 2021

EULOGY

He was the bright light in my sky.
All the brilliant colours of the earth.

This was a man
Good, brave and true
Of strong, unwavering Faith.
When first we met, he said,
"I'm open, direct, broadminded."
And he was all of those.
He loved to shock.
He had a quirky sense of humour.
He was a wicked tease.
He had great charm and courtesy
And he was greatly loved,
Not just as a priest but also as a loving friend.

He had his darker side.
(Who of us does not?)
He could be obstinate, *so* obstinate,
Impatient and sometimes very prickly.
He could be selfish, too,
Just like the rest of us.
For me, it made him human.
I loved him for himself.

He wasn't ready yet to go,
Still making plans ahead.
But I am thankful that he died the way he did
Before he needed care.
Wheelchair-bound or in a home.
His fiercely independent nature
Would have *hated* that.
He was a very private man.

The light has faded from my sky,
Muted the colours of the earth.
Now I am lost.

July 2021

UNTITLED

Just as with my lost treasures,
I must remember you the way I do them.
Know that for the time that is left to me
I must grasp the knowledge that you'll never leave me.

Invisible, intangible, you'll still be there
Inside my heart and mind.

August 2021

ACKNOWLEDGEMENTS

My grateful thanks to Irene Beager, who was my proofreader.

And to the splendid team at Matador, who, as always, produced a high-quality finished work.